ACTON AS IT WAS

A selection of photographs compiled and annotated by
London Borough of Ealing Library Service and R. N. G. Rowland

First Edition, November 1981
Second Impression, April 1987
Third Impression, May 1993

Published by: Hendon Publishing Co. Ltd., Hendon Mill, Nelson, Lancashire.
Text © London Borough of Ealing Library Service 1981
Printed by Peter Fretwell & Sons Ltd., Healey Works, Goulbourne Street, Keighley, West Yorkshire BD21 1PZ.

INTRODUCTION

In this book we illustrate places and personalities from the history of Acton over several hundred years.

The book itself would not exist without the enthusiasm and unstinting help given by a life long Acton resident, Mr R. N. G. Rowland. It is Mr Rowland's work on the resources of the Local History Collection coupled with his encyclopaedic knowledge of Acton which is the backbone of this publication: he made the initial selection of material, identified people and places, provided names and dates, and wrote the captions in his informative and entertaining style. If proof were needed of his credentials for the job, I would refer readers to Mr Rowland's other writings on Acton, and to Plate 7 in this book, where our colleague is shown, at two years of age, with his father outside the family business in Berrymead Gardens in 1914. Thanks are also due to Mr K. L. M. Gwynn for his technical help.

The arrangement of the illustrations is such that we are taken along the Uxbridge Road from east to west, then along Horn Lane into North Acton, and finally through South Acton, Acton Green and East Acton.

The history of Acton is long. Archaeological remains show sporadic human settlement in the area from around 300,000 B.C. At some time in the Dark Ages Anglo-Saxon settlers gave the area the name Actun, or 'oak settlement'. The name Actone ('the farm by the Oak Trees') was first recorded in 1181, when it appeared in St. Paul's Domesday. The character of Acton until late in the nineteenth century was largely agricultural, although times were not necessarily uneventful.

The Black Death visited Acton in 1348 and the Great Plague in 1665; and these and other epidemics helped to keep the population small (about 400 people around 1540) and its growth slow. In November 1642 Acton Green was the scene of an engagement between King Charles's army and the Parliamentary forces under the Earl of Essex and General Skippon. In the eighteenth century Acton enjoyed a brief fame as a fashionable watering place, with Acton Wells acquiring assembly rooms, and in the season the neighbouring hamlets of Friars Place and East Acton teemed with persons of rank.

Acton's growth in the later nineteenth century was spectacular: what we might nowadays call a population explosion. The population, still only 2,500 in 1851, had by 1871 reached 8,000; yet by 1881 it was over 17,000 and by 1901 it exceeded 37,000. A factor in this growth was the reapportionment of medieval strip holdings on Acton's four common fields as a result of the Enclosure Commissioner's Award of 1859, and the requirement for metalled and sewered roads across these fields: this gave the opportunity for development. In addition London was spreading; Bedford Park, England's first garden suburb, was established: a considerable hand laundry industry grew up (Plate 55), giving Acton the nick-name 'the wash-tub of London'.

Acton had its own Local Board from 1866, and in 1895 it became an urban district.

The twentieth century saw the arrival of modern industry, at first in Acton Vale; between the Wars big industrial estates appeared in the north, astride the new Western Avenue. The town's growing importance was recognised by its incorporation as a Borough in 1921. It was a proud boast of the Chamber of Commerce in the 1930s that Acton was the biggest manufacturing town south of Coventry.

At the time of its amalgamation into the London Borough of Ealing in 1965 Acton had a population of almost 70,000. Mr Rowland observes that Acton retains its identity through its parliamentary representation, the transport and postal authorities, and 'the commonsense usage of the man-in-the-street'. He has no fear that that identity will be lost.

I said in a companion volume, *Ealing As It Was* (1980), that individual items of local history can disappear, sometimes overnight. I repeat the invitation to anyone with photographs, drawings, paintings or printed material relevant to the history of the Borough to contact the Local History Librarian, who will be pleased to receive items, as gifts or loans for copying, to extend the collection represented in this book.

Andrew J. C. Scott
Principal Reference Librarian.

1. The tollgate in The Vale near the end of Crown Lane (Bromyard Avenue) functioned until 1872. Over the trees is the roof of the King's Arms, moved westward from here to the corner of East Acton Lane in 1884.

2. The windmill, at what is now the north-west corner of the bowling green in Acton Park, survived until the mid-nineteenth century. The miller then was William Billington whose family name was still remembered until the Steyne clearances of the 1960s did away with Billington Place. The land for the park was acquired by the Local Board in 1888.

3. Berrymead is first documented about 1220–30. It was held from then until 1544 by St. Paul's Cathedral, being perhaps leased into secular hands. After that it was owned by numerous members of the nobility and gentry. In 1802 what was then a very plain building was embellished with battlements and turrets, in the fashionable romantic style, and fancifully renamed The Priory. The estate was built up in the 1880s but the house remained as a Constitutional Club and then as an annexe to a great bakery adjoining. At the time of writing it lies derelict in Salisbury Street, and its fate hangs in the balance.

4. In 1712, when Berrymead was occupied by the Duke of Kingston, his daughter Lady Mary Pierrepoint eloped from there with the diplomat Edward Wortley Montague. He became ambassador to Turkey; she, under her married name, became famous as an oriental traveller and letterwriter, and poses here in appropriate costume. She brought the practice of inoculation for smallpox from Turkey to England.

5. The site of Grove House, opposite the Town Hall, is now occupied by the Technical College. From 1896 a boys' private school, Acton College, was here, first under Mr E. C. Sunnuck and then from 1912 under Dr John Mackey, In 1925 the school moved into our sister-suburb and became Ealing College. Out of view on the right were more classrooms and a vast playground. In hard winters pupils skated on the pond—after the ice had been tested by some wretched usher deputed by the headmaster.

6. The Town Hall of 1939 stands on the site of the King George V garden, here being opened on Coronation Day 1911. After the First World War army recruiting huts here accommodated overflow staff from the Council Offices. The public baths' tank advertises its artesian well.

7. No. 1a (later 1) Berrymead Gardens in 1914. Under wartime pressures the business was taken over in 1917 by Long & Pocock, part of the dairy 'combine'. (One of their barrows is in the Gunnersbury Park Museum). With its seventeen-gallon churn of milk, and other impedimenta, a barrow made herculean demands on the roundsman who pushed it about the streets twice or sometimes thrice a day.

8.   Midway down Oldham Terrace St. Mary's school for boys and girls functioned from 1852 to 1934; it was replaced by an Employment Exchange in 1936. The infants' school of 1837 is now in commercial use at the north end of Oldham Terrace.

9. High Street looking east about 1885, approaching the Elephant and Castle, with the trees of the Berrymead grounds in the distance. On the left are Lichfield and Suffolk Houses, built about 1729 and lived in by members of the Garrick family (but *not* by the celebrated actor himself). The gentleman in the white jacket has also sought immortality in the next picture.

10. High Street looking west about 1885. On the left is part of the Berrymead estate wall, then the corner of Oldham Terrace with the Elephant and Castle. On the right are the grounds of Suffolk House where, in 1921, shops and the Globe (later Gaumont) Cinema were built. The latter was replaced by the Precinct in 1966, soon after Lichfield and Suffolk Houses had also disappeared.

11. High Street, a few yards east of Church Road, rebuilt in 1904. On the right is The Wellington, next is Mrs Seymour's dame-school, and on the left is the tuck-shop, the resort of the boys of Mr Mullens's school which, until it was burnt down in the 1850s, stood almost opposite.

12. The north side of High Street in the 1890s. At the corner of Market Place the dummy stone jars, bright red or green, proclaim the oilmen's trade carried on by Messrs. Davies & Evans. Among a multiplicity of other things they also sold tea. The taller block on the right was Beauchamp's Acton Market which included a grocery, bakery, butcher's and fishmonger's.

It is a pity that our High Street has lost its trees.

13. The George and Dragon in the High Street dates from the early seventeenth century. A landlord of the 1840s, Martin Oldham, built and gave his name to the row of cottages in Oldham Terrace which were swept away in 1972. The curious arrangement of 'interlacing' tramtracks, resorted to at the narrower parts of the route, obviated the need for installing points. This view was taken about 1905.

14. This evocative view shows the Orange Tree in the High Street opposite the George and Dragon. It and the buildings to its left were pulled down in 1884. In the photograph the hands of St. Mary's clock point to twenty past two. This gives support to the once-popular notion that the clock was never right, for the shadows of the policeman and the loungers suggest that it is really early evening on a sunny spring or autumn day. The clock behaves itself very much better nowadays.

15. The corner of Mill Hill Grove in 1904, when Mr Warren and Mr Beck themselves, waistcoated and alpaca-sleeved, stood behind their counters. The shop expanded, and threw out branches in Southall and Greenford; it is now a Co-operative Retail Store.

16. This view of the High Street *circa* 1890 looks from the corner of Mill Hill Grove towards Acton Hill. Mount Terrace, on the right, was pulled down in 1893–94, leaving an open triangle in front of St. Mary's church; at the same time the King's Head, whose sign overhangs the road, was set back. On the left, T. Baker's Stores, a delightful 'traditional' provision shop, survived until 1963. Its fine building, Mitre House, was once the home of William Lloyd, Bishop of Norwich, who as a non-juror was deprived under William III. The shops beyond this were rebuilt in 1901–10.

17. High Street, facing The Mount, in the 1890s. The house on the left was occupied by Richard Baxter, the nonconformist divine, in the 1660s and 70s. It was demolished in 1901; the rest went soon after. It is to Mr Upjohn, next door, that we owe so many photographs of Acton at that time.

18. Continuation westward of the preceding view. On the right is the Six Bells, rebuilt in 1910, with the arched entrance to Cock and Crown Yard.

19.   Cock and Crown Yard recalls the Cock tavern, known to have existed in 1636. It was approached through an arched entry by the Six Bells. Its notorious squalor is here under scrutiny by two visitants from bureaucratic heights; this must have been only one of many inspections which resulted in its being replaced by Crown Street in 1910.

20.   A Plaistow-to-Ealing London General bus passes the King's Head in 1909. The building on the left is about to be demolished to make way for Crown Street. The notice on the tram-standard advises that 'Electric cars stop here'.

21. High Street *circa* 1890 from the foot of Acton Hill. The King's Head, whose sign overhangs the road, was set back in 1894. On the left is Virginia House, which became Messrs. Poore's shop when they moved from Mount Terrace. On the right is Mr Morgan the jeweller's public timepiece, which was still marking the passing hours in the 1930s.

22. In the 1890s Mr A. T. Overall, at 238 High Street, displays his saddles, whips, horse-collars and sundry leatherware. The business is still in family hands, and one of the few in Acton trading under its 'old-time' name—but no longer selling 'Molliscorium' embrocation.

23. *Town Acton 1799* by R. Hollogan looks at the High Street from the foot of Acton Hill, where the road once forded the Stamford Brook. The archway on the left probably leads to Bank House in the Steyne, which was pulled down in 1870.

24. The same view in 1885. Covering the Bank House estate are shops and the 1871 offices of the Local Board. The Council moved to Winchester Street in 1910, but the offices housed private firms until demolition in the early 1930s made room for the Steyne junction to be re-formed. The cock-horse boy waits for a driver seeking extra horsepower to help his vehicle up Acton Hill.

25. Just after 1901, at the Acton Hill corner of Gunnersbury Lane: the Pineapple and the Old Red Lion. The entrance to Gunnersbury Lane was then half its present inadequate width, and in 1906–7 these twin pubs were rebuilt, with a set-back corner, as the Red Lion. Behind the tree, right, is the yard of the London United Tramways depot of 1895, still used by London Transport.

26. A horse-tramway from Shepherds Bush reached Berrymead lodge gates in 1878. Passing into the vigorous management of the London United company it pushed on to the top of Acton Hill, seen here, in 1894. In 1901 it was electrified and extended to Southall. A standard for overhead electric wires shows above the top deck of the car, so these horses are about to enjoy a grassy retirement. The smart uniforms of driver and conductor testify to L.U.T.'s efficiency.

27. *Above left:* At the time this picture was taken the house on the right was Acton's oldest building. It stood at 300 High Street, opposite the tram depot. The inscribed stone between the upper windows, now in the Gunnersbury Park Museum, reads: 'Mary's Place, built 1588, restored 1873'. This view was taken shortly before Mary's Place was demolished in 1932.

28. *Above right:* One of the last surviving great houses of Acton, The Elms, stands at the top of Acton Hill. It was built in 1735 for Sir Joseph Ayloffe, Keeper of the Record Office, and from 1749 until 1842 was held by the Wegg family. A Victorian occupant was James Shoolbred, owner of the once famous great stores in Tottenham Court Road. It is now part of the Twyford C. of E. High School.

29. *Below right:* Acton's most renamed road is an ancient track leading to West Twyford. Once called Green Lane or Mill Lane, its winding southern end was straightened in 1759 by the landowner, Samuel Wegg of The Elms, and was then called the New Road. Towards the end of the last century, the date of our view, it became Wegg Avenue and then, on being developed about 1901, Twyford Avenue.

30. Commemorated by Hale Gardens, L.C.J. Sir Matthew Hale lived in Acton from 1667 until shortly before his death in 1676. Richard Baxter, the nonconformist divine, also lived here at the time, out of favour with the Establishment, but remarkably he and Hale became close friends.

31. Gunnersbury Lane, approaching Acton Hill, on a sunny morning about 1890. The 1938 fire station now stands right of the lamp-post.

32. A late Victorian view of Gunnersbury Lane, looking towards Mill Hill Park station, renamed Acton Town in 1910. The trees on the right conceal Heathfield Lodge, demolished in 1969, and Avenue Road debouches on the left.

33. Until 1868 Acton's only means of fire-fighting was by human bucket-chain. Engines from Ealing and Hammersmith had to deal with serious outbreaks so the Local Board acquired this manual pump, which lasted until steam pumps arrived in 1899. At this display at Syon Park in 1871, the gallant volunteers on top of the engine are, left to right, Harmer, Vaughan, Rolfe, Elmer, Eydmann, Poore and Lowman (captain). Richardson (with rosette) is seated left, and Dunn stands on the right.

34. Before the redevelopment of 1893–94 Messrs. Poore had a shop on Mount Terrace and this warehouse in King Street. Master William Poore and his brother have been entrusted with the pony-trap. On the left is the old King's Head. The fly-posted building, right, disappeared in the widening of King Street.

35. When this picture was taken in the 1880s King Street had been known by its present name for many years, but we see clearly why it was once called Back Lane. On the extreme left is the entrance to Church Passage, then only a footpath. The buildings from here to the High Street were swept away in 1893–94 to form the open triangle in front of St. Mary's. The distant pedimented building facing the camera is the Acton Bon Marché on the south side of the High Street, where the ladies flocked to buy their bonnets, ribbons and furbelows.

36. St. Mary's church from the north-east about 1800. This mainly medieval structure was 'improved' over succeeding years with the addition of a classical porch and other incongruous features.

37. The body of St. Mary's church was rebuilt in 1866, but the medieval tower remained until 1877, so for eleven years the church presented this hybrid appearance. It may be that we are witnessing here the widening of the entrance to Churchfield Road in 1873.

38. *Above left:* A notable centenarian of a notable family, William Aldridge, wheelwright, was buried in St. Mary's in 1698, in his 115th year. If he was born in Acton this would mean Aldridges lived here for some 300 years. Later members of the family acted as parish clerks.

39. *Above right:* St. Mary's Rectory, in the angle of Horn Lane and Rectory Road, is on a site that has probably accommodated the parsonage from time immemorial. Acton's first rector known by name took office in 1228; the record of his predecessors is lost. The house seen here was built in 1725, and it was replaced by the present rectory in 1925.

40. *Below right:* Steyne comes from an Old English word meaning 'stony'. East Row, shown here, faced Horn Lane; since 1939 Steyne House flats have been on the site.

41. *Above left:* Derwentwater House stood in Horn Lane opposite the Steyne; this is its east front. Lord Mayor Sir Henry Garraway had a house here in the 1630s. In 1720 it was leased to the Countess of Derwentwater whose husband, a Jacobite rebel, had been beheaded in 1716. Intending to stay in Acton, she gave the house her own name, but within a year she moved to Brussels and died shortly afterwards. The house was rebuilt early in the nineteenth century, its grounds were developed around 1905, and it was pulled down in 1909.

42. *Above:* Jack Whitehorn, the youthful roundsman from Mr T. Willy's shop at 100 Churchfield Road, is about to make a delivery at 2 Pierrepoint Road (now replaced by Magnolia Lodge). Tommy the pony was stabled in Spencer Road, behind the Congregational Church. The year is about 1910. (Information kindly given by Mr Tom Willy Jnr.)

43. *Below left:* Horn Lane in the 1880s looking north. On the right are the grounds of The Lodge, home of the cricketing Beldam family, and Apsley Terrace is in the distance. Since 1934 Springfield Gardens park has been on the left here.

44. To take this view of Horn Lane in the 1860s the photographer stood at what is now the corner of Creswick Road, looking towards North Acton. The army drill hall now stands on the left here; the building in the picture is the lodge of 'Shalimar', which lies out of view behind the further trees. The distant white railings guard the hollow in which flows the Stamford Brook, west branch, on its course to the Thames at Hammersmith.

45. 'Shalimar' faced the top end of Shalimar Gardens. The grounds between it and Horn Lane were developed in the 1880s, but the house survived, as a school for young ladies, just into the new century. Some of the Pakenham family once lived here; perhaps their Indo-military connections suggested the exotic name of the house.

46. Opposite Apsley Terrace in Horn Lane on Wednesday 26 June 1912 two charming teenagers rattle their collecting tins on this first-ever Alexandra Rose Day (one can just make out the Queen's head on the tins). Those who marvel at Beauchamp's offering Danish butter at 1s. 2d. (say 6p) a pound should reflect that a week's wages will buy much more butter today than in 1912.

47. A great rainstorm on Derby Day 1911 inundated much of West London. Here is the flood in Horn Lane, as seen from the corner of Essex Road. It would appear that mother has recommended the wearing of father's Wellington boots.

48. The Great Western Railway's Acton Station (renamed Acton Main Line in 1949) was opened in 1869, thirty one years after the building of the line. The extra rails seen here allow the running of standard gauge trains as well as the broad gauge used by the G.W.R. until 1892. When this picture was taken in the 1870s Acton's population was rocketing; boards on the platforms advertise 'Houses to let close to this station'.

49. *Above left:* Before Victoria Road was made in 1901 the green partly seen on the right made a dog-leg angle between Horn Lane and Park Royal Road. This was the original Gipsy Corner, and travellers' caravans halted here into the 1920s; it now accommodates a public convenience. Mr Tomes the stonemason stands at the roadside; much of the family's handiwork adorns the then new cemetery of 1893 on the left.

50. *Above:* Friars Place stood on land acquired in the fourteenth century by St. Bartholomew the Great, Smithfield. Nobody knows whether there ever was a religious house here; all that is certain is that the house in this view was vacated by Henry Emanuel about 1885 and fell into ruin. In 1920–21 Messrs. T. Wall built their plant on the site, and named it The Friary.

51. *Below left:* Acton Aerodrome, the scene of much pioneer flying, lay in the triangle now formed by Masons Green Lane, Western Avenue and Saxon Drive. To its north was the Park Royal airfield, seen here at 5 a.m. on 23 April 1910, with Claude Grahame White about to begin his first attempt to fly to Manchester.

52. This intrepid sportsman of about 1870, with his boneshaker and display of trophies, is Charlie Gee, a scion of the family who owned the Steyne Mills. He is said to have been a high-spirited lad and a great contriver of practical jokes. And who, on the evidence of this picture, can doubt it?

53. Forty years on, and in Church Road about 1910 Charlie Gee has attained the dignity of being Mr. Cllr. J. C. Gee. The Messrs. Tilley, who contribute so much to this inspired black-and-white study, and their handcart, were familiar sights about the streets of Acton almost until the Second World War.

54. Church Road, then about 40 years old, looking north at the turn of the century. Halfway up on the right is Acton Hall, a venue for all kinds of gatherings, sacred and secular. The attraction advertised here is 'Restaurant Concert 8 p.m. Saturday'. Acton's first cinematograph shows were given here. The hall and most of Church Road have been lost in recent clearances.

55. When Turnham Field was being developed as South Acton in the 1860s there was a great influx of people from overcrowded Notting Dale. Many of them had managed, or worked in, laundries, and in a few years their new home had become 'Soapsuds Island', the washtub of London.

By the turn of the century there were 180 laundries, great and small, in South Actorr. Here is the staff of one of the more substantial establishments, off for a day's spree, perhaps to Ruislip Ponds or even further afield.

56. The more things change . . . perhaps our notorious weather has forced them indoors on this Edwardian May Day at the Berrymede infants' school in Osborne Road.

57. The dignified All Saints' Church in Bollo Bridge Road (by J. Kelly and M. B. Adams) was consecrated in 1872. Edward Monson added a south-east chapel in 1895, and the spire was lost in a Second World War air raid. The church had not been built long when this photograph was taken. The hayfield was mentioned in evidence at the trial of the murderer of P.C. William Davey, shot in Avenue Road in 1863.

58. At the corner of Cleveland Road and Church Path *circa* 1900 Mr Stokes the cartage contractor proudly shows off his team, decorated for a horse-show.

59. Chiswick Park and Acton Green station in 1906, soon after the District Railway was electrified. It began life in 1879 as Acton Green; after various jugglings with its name it is now Chiswick Park. It was rebuilt in 1931–32.

60. The Duke of Sussex, at the corner of South Parade and Beaconsfield Road, before it was rebuilt in 1898. The group of thirsters after Superior Porter and Old Tom Gin wear a typical selection of the clumsy trouserings of the period. But the lamps add panache.

61. Dr John Lindley (1797–1865) lived at Bedford House (Bedford Park) and Fairlawn (Acton Green). He founded the *Gardener's Chronicle*, was first Professor of Botany at London University, and was instrumental in having Kew Gardens made over to the nation as a world-centre of botanical science with easy access for the public. He is buried in the Churchfield Road graveyard.

62. A garden studio in the late 1860s in the newly completed Shakespeare Road. The saucy-hatted young lady distracts the eye from the cornfield in what is now Woodhurst Road.

North London Station, Acton.

63. The Churchfield Road level crossing early in this century. Here is Acton's first railway station, opened in 1853 and rebuilt in 1875. The line was officially the N. & S.W. Junction Railway; it was served by North London trains and electrified in 1916. Note the clerestory on the guard's van roof giving a clear view fore and aft over the train.

64. The smithy in East Acton Lane stood just north of Shaa Road. It shut up shop in 1909, but the buildings stayed here until the present houses were built some 20 years later.

Smithy at East Acton.

65. When John Perryn, a goldsmith from Bromyard in Worcestershire, died in 1657 he left his great house and its extensive lands in East Acton to the Goldsmiths' Company. The house was rebuilt early in the next century, but it fell into decay after the 1880s and was pulled down in 1911. It stood very near East Acton Lane, on the right of the drive now leading to the Manor House sports grounds.

66. The Goldsmiths' Arms at East Acton, before it was rebuilt in 1910. Next to it is the village store (also at that time a post office), pulled down in 1964 to make room for a car-park. The Council's watercarts were refilled from the standpipe, centre. To the left of this is a fire-alarm post—'Break glass, pull knob and wait for engines'.